This Journal Belongs to

....

Contact Information

....

....

....

Date

....

Ellie Claire
Hachette Book Group
1290 Avenue of the Americas, New York, NY 10104
ellieclaire.com

First Edition: September 2022.

Ellie Claire is a division of Hachette Book Group, Inc.
The Ellie Claire name and logo are trademarks of Hachette Book Group, Inc.
The publisher is not responsible for websites (or their content) that are not owned by the publisher.

Unless otherwise noted, the quotes in this book were taken from Joel Osteen's *Rule Your Day*.

Print book interior design by Bart Dawson.

ISBN: 9781546002864

Printed in China
APS
10 9 8 7 6 5 4 3 2 1

God is going to
make things *happen*
that you didn't
see coming.

Introduction

You would like to savor each moment, grow into your best life, engage in productive relationships, and see your dreams come to pass. But distractions, delays, and disappointments relentlessly hijack your plans and undermine your good intentions. While you can't control everything that comes your way, you can control how life's unexpected setbacks affect your attitude, emotions, thoughts, and actions.

Along with the book *Rule Your Day*, this journal is meant to help you mind your mind-set and claim control over each new day. Discover encouraging, inspirational thoughts from the book that serve as daily reminders of how to identify faulty thinking, recast your vision for the future, and rise above your circumstances. All are provided to engage you in a process of reflection that will help you guard your heart and mind against negativity and transcend distractions to focus on what matters most.

Let this be an open door to self-discovery and a record of your daily progress as you begin to take control of your day. You can bounce back from disappointments, prevent poisonous thoughts from entering your atmosphere, and fully enjoy the bright future that's ahead of you. Don't settle for surviving when you could be thriving.

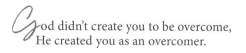

God didn't create you to be overcome,
He created you as an overcomer.

You have to be careful what you allow in. You can't stop every negative thing from coming, but you can stop it from getting down in your spirit.

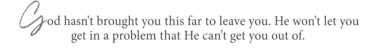

God hasn't brought you this far to leave you. He won't let you get in a problem that He can't get you out of.

....
....
....
....
....
....
....
....
....
....
....
....
....
....
....
....
....
....
....
....
....
....
....
....
....

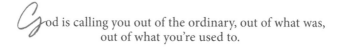

God is calling you out of the ordinary, out of what was, out of what you're used to.

If it's not positive, hopeful, and of a good report, don't dwell on it. You can't control the whole world, but you can control your atmosphere.

*Y*ou're going to become what you're continually saying.

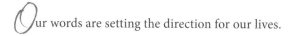

Our words are setting the direction for our lives.

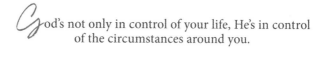

God's not only in control of your life, He's in control
of the circumstances around you.

You haven't seen, heard, or imagined where God is taking you.

You can't be silent and reach your potential.

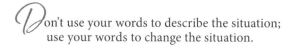

*Don't use your words to describe the situation;
use your words to change the situation.*

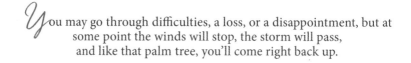

You may go through difficulties, a loss, or a disappointment, but at some point the winds will stop, the storm will pass, and like that palm tree, you'll come right back up.

*A*re you letting God arise or are you letting the problem arise?

When you help others, what you give is going to come back to you not in the same proportion, but pressed down and running over.

That seed you're sowing is going to keep coming back to you.

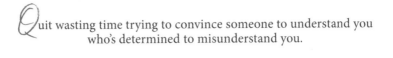
*Q*uit wasting time trying to convince someone to understand you who's determined to misunderstand you.

You weren't created to be controlled by others, to not be able to pursue your dreams and have time to do what God put in your heart.

As you help someone else shine, God is going to make sure that you shine.

Everyone has a right to have their opinion, and you have the right not to take it.

It's very freeing when you realize you're not responsible for keeping other people happy.

....

....

....

....

....

....

....

....

....

....

....

....

....

....

....

....

....

....

....

....

....

....

....

....

You can't soar with the eagles if you're hanging around with the chickens.

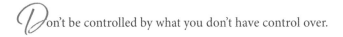

Don't be controlled by what you don't have control over.

When you make sacrifices to help other people's dreams come to pass, God will help make your dream come to pass.

Life is hard enough without adding negative things that make it more difficult.

Create a lifestyle where you develop the habit of speaking health, speaking favor, speaking abundance.

Don't sit inactive with people who don't believe in you, with people who don't come into agreement with your dream.

*A*re you sending your words out in the direction you want your life to go?

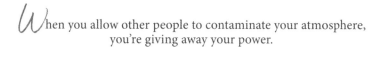

*W*hen you allow other people to contaminate your atmosphere,
you're giving away your power.

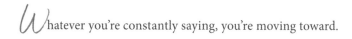

Whatever you're constantly saying, you're moving toward.

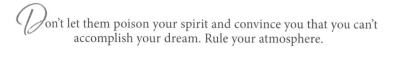

*D*on't let them poison your spirit and convince you that you can't accomplish your dream. Rule your atmosphere.

You believe what you say about yourself more than what anyone else says.

....
....
....
....
....
....
....
....
....
....
....
....
....
....
....
....
....
....
....
....
....
....
....
....

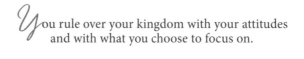

You rule over your kingdom with your attitudes and with what you choose to focus on.

God has daily favor, daily wisdom, daily ideas,
daily abundance. If you stay open,
He'll lead you into the fullness of your destiny.

God has called you to leave your mark, to take your family to a new level.

Just because it was right in the past doesn't mean it's right for today.

If you do your part and control what you can control,
if you rule your atmosphere, your thoughts,
and your attitudes, then God will do His part.

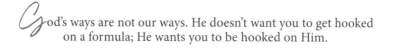

God's ways are not our ways. He doesn't want you to get hooked on a formula; He wants you to be hooked on Him.

....

....

....

....

....

....

....

....

....

....

....

....

....

....

....

....

....

....

....

....

....

....

....

You can't control all that's around you, but you can control what gets in you. Are your walls up? Are you ruling your spirit?

You can't rely on what got you to where you are to keep you where you are.